Timber Iron Clay

TIMBER
IRON
CLAY five essays on their use in building

Derek Linstrum
Alec Clifton-Taylor
Martin Opie
Barrie Trinder
Ronald Brunskill

a West Midlands Arts publication

Copyright © 1975
West Midlands Arts
Lloyd's Bank Chambers
Market Street
Stafford
ST16 2AP

ISBN 9 504 3640 2

Designed by Rachel Davies
Photographs by Colin Reiners
final year BA students
North Staffordshire Polytechnic
Department of Graphic Design and Printing
Design tutor Graham Stevens MSIA

Set in 10pt 'Monophoto' Plantin, series 110 and 194

Made and Printed in Great Britain by
Wood Mitchell and Company Limited, Stoke-on-Trent
ST7 2AD

Contents

Avoncroft Museum of Buildings.

Ironbridge Gorge Museum.

Preface

The idea of drawing together this collection of essays grew, in the first place, out of an exhibition project – *TIMBER IRON CLAY* – by which West Midlands Arts, in conjunction with Avoncroft Museum of Buildings, Ironbridge Gorge Museum and Gladstone Pottery Museum celebrated European Architectural Heritage Year.

This little 'festschrift', if one may call it such, is however published very much in its own right as an attempt to assemble a view of the past and present use, including the conservational aspect of the three materials – *TIMBER IRON CLAY* – not only as building materials, but, in the cases of iron and clay in particular, as the raw materials upon which much of the development of the Midlands has been based.

The editors of the book, whose editing has necessarily been minimal and whose enjoyment in the task enormous, wish me to express their very great thanks here to the contributors for deciphering so perceptively what was needed, and for extending to us their knowledge of and

Gladstone Pottery Museum.
Sketches from the sites of each museum
by Sir Hugh Casson.

enthusiasm for their particular subjects. The editors are also especially grateful to Sir Hugh Casson for so kindly providing us with sketches related to the Museum sites for use in publicity and design.

I should, in turn, like to thank the editors, Michael Thomas, Director of Avoncroft Museum of Buildings, Neil Cossons, Director of Ironbridge Gorge Museum, David Sekers, Director of Gladstone Pottery Museum, and David Rees, Chairman of West Midlands Arts Craft Advisory Group, for watching over every stage of the project and applying seemingly limitless knowledge and practical help to the compilation of material for the book.

Finally, everyone concerned with the project will, I feel sure, want to give sincere thanks for the work of the staff and students in the Graphic Design and Printing Department of the North Staffordshire Polytechnic, and in particular to Rachel Davies for the overall design of the book and to Colin Reiners for many of the photographs.

We hope that the book will give as much enjoyment to all who read it as it has to us in presenting it.

Lisa Henderson, MA
Visual Arts and Crafts Officer
West Midlands Arts

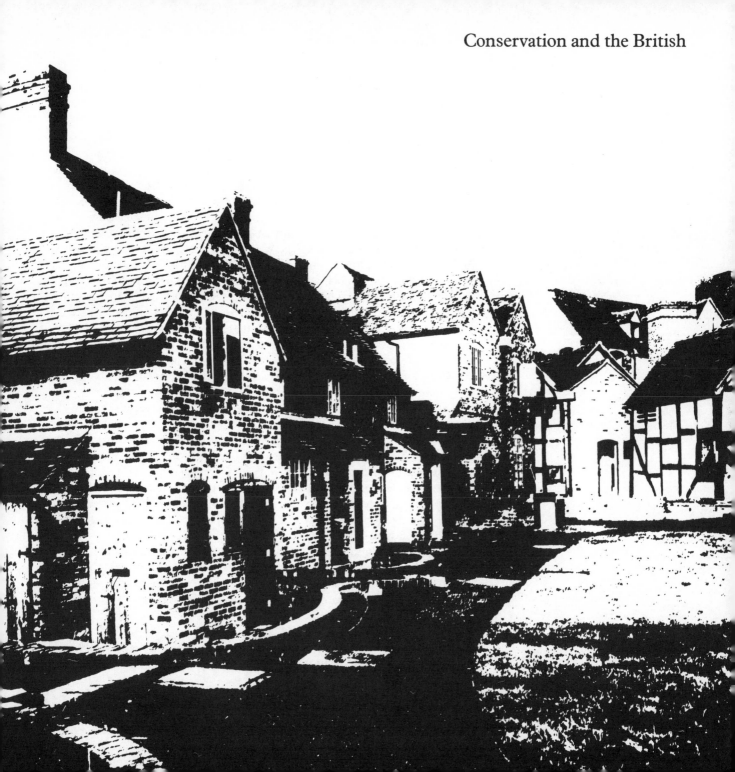

Conservation and the British

Derek Linstrum

'Past and to come seem best; things present, worst', said Sir John Falstaff, proving himself a philosopher. The worse the present, the more we look to the past and the future; and as few seem able to look with great confidence today to the future, so there is a strong inclination to retreat and hold on to what is familiar. It is in that light that we must see the general attitude to the buildings remaining from the past. It may not be entirely new; for the last hundred years there has been legislation designed to protect ancient monuments, and during that time a number of organisations have been founded with ever wider aims in their concern for preserving buildings from the past; the Society for the Protection of Ancient Buildings, the National Trust, the Ancient Monuments Society, the Council for British Archaeology, the Georgian Group, the Victorian Society, the Civic Trust, and many hundreds of local civic societies and residents' associations dedicated to safeguarding whatever *they* choose to regard as *their* heritage. It is an impressive illustration of a regard for the past which cannot be dismissed as merely nostalgia. Maybe it can be explained by a deeply rooted conservatism in the British character and an adherence to living, continuous traditions; but is that too facile an explanation of the present prevalence of talk about conservation?

What *is* conservation? My own definition is that conservation is the ensuring of the continuity of life into an undefined future. The means by which this is done in architecture are various; preservation, restoration, maintenance, rehabilitation, adaptation, even reconstruction. But why exactly do we believe there is value in certain buildings? Can we define value? Visual? Human? Economic? Political? Is it possible to quantify all, or any, of these? Of course we can quote the father of British conservation, William Morris, who told us quite simply, 'these old buildings do not belong to us only; . . . they belonged to our forefathers and they will belong to our descendants unless we play them false. They are not in any sense our property, to do as we like with them. We are only trustees for those that come after us.'

That is a moving description. It is a declaration of faith in the past and the future, that leaves one feeling spiritually uplifted and impressed with a sense of responsibility; but it is not particularly practical advice today when we can seldom think of a building in isolation. Indeed, the outstanding characteristic of our present thinking about conservation is that we are concerned about the totality of a place, and not with individual items.

Yet most of the incentives to conserve come, in the first place, from concern for an individual building, and there are recognised criteria for deciding whether or not to add one to the statutory list of buildings of architectural and historic importance. It might be a work of art in itself which enriches the environment, or one of special value within certain types for architectural or planning reasons, or as illustrating some aspect

1 Malt Mill Lane, Alcester, Warwickshire. Associated Architects. This imaginative conservation project received an EAHY award for Exceptional Merit 1975.

of social or economic history; it might be one which displays technological innovation or virtuosity, or one which is representative of its time; it might be one associated with well-known characters or events; or it might be one which possesses group value in town planning terms – a definition capable of wide interpretation. These criteria are probably similar to those applied in most other countries in which there is a system of listing for protection; but the way in which they are interpreted, legally, administratively and visually, must be conditioned by national attitudes and resources. Is it possible to identify the British approach?

The answer is complex, but one aspect is that although there is considerable State aid there is relatively little *direct* State control. Another is that the idea of conservation as an element in planning and design is becoming widely accepted in theory. Then we might wonder if those supposedly British characteristics of conservatism and respect for tradition encourage conservation; and there is the love of the 'Picturesque', inherent in a British appreciation of art and architecture. But above all there is the pervasive influence of the public and the wide spread of an active concern for our architectural heritage; in that lies the great strength of conservation as a creative force in this country, and one without parallel elsewhere.

When we consider the simple question of who owns our historic buildings we can see examples of more than one of these elements in the British approach to conservation. The cathedrals and churches which dominate the mass and skyline of most towns are the property of the Church and at present receive no State aid. This means that a whole organisation of architects, clergy and voluntary workers is responsible for the largest single category of historic building. The continuity of a church depends on the work of the parish and involves the community in its widest sense. The recent restoration of York Minster was accomplished because more than £2 000 000 was subscribed by individuals, industrialists and local government authorities, and the work was rightly regarded as a corporate, not a State, responsibility. St Paul's Cathedral appealed for

£3 000 000 in 1971, and only this year Canterbury Cathedral has asked for £3 500 000. Churches, too, are continually in need of money for maintenance and conservation; and once again there is no State aid but a direct involvement with the community. It is a British paradox that only when a church has become officially dead and redundant is it possible to obtain money to help it, but the result is a healthy spreading of the responsibility for conservation. Similarly, the National Trust's ownership of country houses and landscape, from the great historic homes to windmills, is a method of public ownership and participation which gives the members of the Trust a feeling of responsibility for historic buildings. Many country houses are owned by local government authorities, generally for use as museums, galleries or educational establishments; some have become privately owned schools, hospitals or homes for the elderly; and it must be remembered that university buildings are the property of individual universities, or, as at Oxford and Cambridge, individual colleges. The State's direct responsibility is for the ruined castles, abbeys and monasteries that can be found in lonely valleys or on the cliffs overlooking the sea, romantic, deserted symbols of our country's history; it also cares for the Royal palaces and other national monuments as well as for government buildings which happen to be historic, but it can be seen that the majority of the 207 643 listed buildings, many of them houses, cottages or farms, are privately owned. Grants are available to help pay for the necessary repairs, but the responsibility for the country's architectural heritage is advantageously spread very wide.

Considering the idea of conservation as an element in planning and design, it is commonly said that no other European country has such powerful, detailed legislation to protect historic buildings as Britain, although it would be dangerous to suggest that is a cause for complacency. The post-war years were devoted to trying to build the brave new world of white towers in green parks which had been the ideal of the generation of architects trained in the 1930s. The first post-war Planning Acts paid little attention to provision for old buildings, with devastating results. The Civic Amenities Act of 1967 added several necessary controls as well as introducing the new idea of the Conservation Area as one of special or architectural interest, possessing an identifiable character which it was desirable to preserve and enhance. The response has been extremely interesting. Around 3 378 Conservation Areas have been designated so far, ranging from those with obvious merit such as the authors of the Act had in mind, to some which to an outsider might seem quite lacking in merit. There have been immediately attractive towns with a picturesque mixture of buildings, nineteenth century leafy suburbs, urban areas in industrial cities, and a few which mysteriously included new shopping centres or speculative housing. The Act has probably worked out slightly differently from what was intended, but it has humanised the legislation by appealing to local pride and introducing the realities of conservation to the inhabitants in the Areas.

It may not be perfect, and we still have to find out how successful it is in operation over a long period; but it is the best answer we have found so far. The change in emphasis can be seen in the successive Government circulars which interpret the Act; the most recent ones refer to the 'cherished local scene' as something to conserve. This is a step in a different direction from one concerned with visual quality, but certainly not one in the wrong direction. More recent legislation in the 1974 Town and Country Planning Act has applied stricter control over demolition of *any* building in a Conservation Area, and over the cutting down or mutilation of trees. New legislation has inevitably brought about a change of attitude in the planning departments, and conservation is now more widely recognised as an element in planning and design. Whole areas which can hardly be considered historic are being looked at more sympathetically, especially those which are predominantly housing. Once we look beyond the monuments, the churches, the public buildings, the great mansions, housing must be our main concern; and that means housing that is well maintained and obviously eminently desirable on every count like the eighteenth century New Town of Edinburgh or sixteenth century cottages in a country town within reach of an urban population; housing that has once been desirable, but which fashion has left behind for various social and economic reasons; housing that was never especially desirable, like the large areas of nineteenth century workers' terraces which still possess virtues and human qualities on account of the communities that have grown up there, and because there is still considerable useful life left in the buildings. We now have an identifiable positive policy of conservation and rehabilitation, of housing action areas, special powers of compulsory improvement, and a welcome tendency to turn away from a policy of comprehensive redevelopment in favour of conservation and a gradual redevelopment on a small scale when necessary. It is a conservative policy which might seem to appeal to the conservative element in the British character.

Certainly, this extension of the interpretation of conservation has also widened to a previously unthinkable scope the idea of participation. It is true there is a long tradition of occasional outbursts of protest about some proposal or other connected with our historic cities. There was a notable example in York in the early nineteenth century when the proposed demolition of the medieval gateways and walls was prevented by the action of a group of citizens. The local archaeological societies helped to keep alive a concern for old buildings, even if they were thought of in a relatively narrow sense as survivals from the Middle Ages. Ruins were an essential part of British romantic literature and art, and elaborately argued philosophies about the nature of the 'Picturesque' occupied connoisseurs in the early nineteenth century. This visual appreciation of antiquity in architecture is firmly rooted in the British attitude to conservation; and it was strong in John Ruskin's passionate interpretation of architectural beauty, 'Its glory is in its Age . . . It is in that golden stain of time, that we are to look for the real light, and colour, and preciousness of architecture'.

It was John Ruskin and William Morris who began to arouse a wider interest in historic buildings, and such successors in the present century as Sir John Betjeman and John Piper have nobly continued the argument on human, visual and emotional lines, until we now accept the presence of *people* in conservation. The number of official organisations concerned has been swollen to an enormous size by the local amenity societies, protest groups and residents' associations formed for a particular reason, probably to fight a particular threat, and then continuing in existence as a useful and valuable means of communication between the public, their elected representatives in local and central government, and the professional officers. It is public protest and active participation that have helped to provide the stimulus to pedestrianise streets so that they are once again pleasant, human places. It has made a stand against the intolerable conditions produced by the increased volume of traffic in city streets, and there have been notable victories recently in the Secretary of State's refusal to sanction new inner ring-roads. By forming housing associations to rehabilitate old houses in central areas, members of the public are helping slowly to bring back civilised life to our towns and cities. And the violent criticism of the common form of urban renewal, which has usually meant total demolition, has brought about a noticeable change in some central and local government attitudes towards commercial developers' proposals. Indeed, the commercial developer himself now sometimes professes to have seen the light of conservation. Whatever we might think of that, it must be said all this adds up to an extremely interesting, essentially British situation in which the future of our architectural heritage is at last becoming one in which the public can participate to ensure that life and architecture continue to be inseparable. It is no longer the limited concern only of antiquarians on the one hand and planners on the other. The treatment of our historic buildings must necessarily be central to that concern, but by now it is something beyond the wildest dreams of the nineteenth century pioneers who began it all; but so is the threat to our environment.

Timber and Brick in the West Midlands

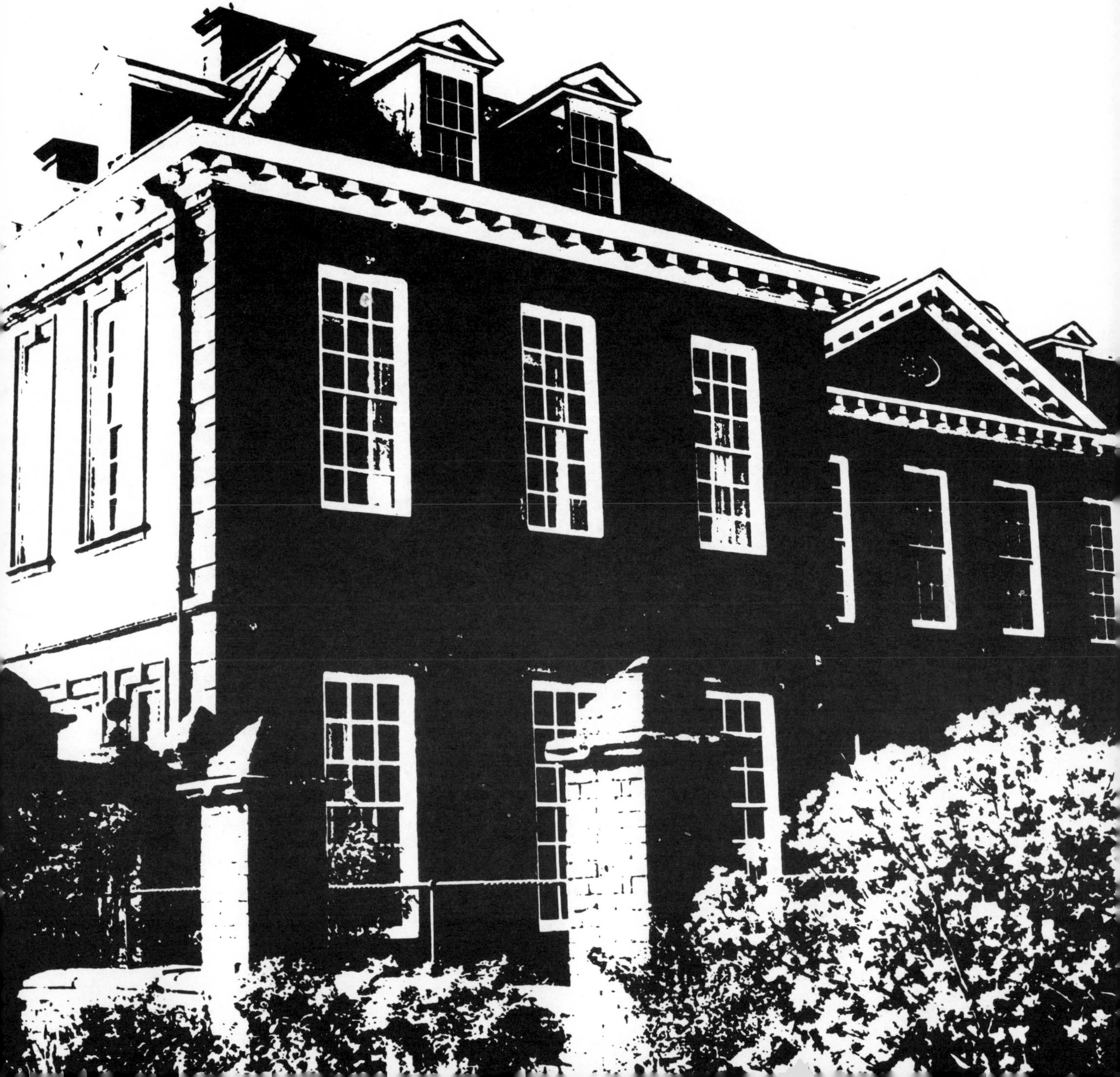

Alec Clifton-Taylor

If the costs of a building are separated under three main headings, the labour, the materials, and the transport of the materials to the site, the last item will nowadays be much the lowest. Before the Industrial Revolution this was not so. The only way to carry heavy materials cheaply was by water. But although for this reason (among others) the majority of old English towns have their river, every building could not be near one. In order to counter the high cost of transport, therefore, people nearly always built with the materials that were at hand locally. Since we are fortunate enough to have a very complex geological structure, this has meant that the pattern of English building is extremely varied.

In the five counties of the West Midlands – Warwickshire, Worcestershire, Staffordshire, Shropshire and Herefordshire (I ignore the recent meddling with traditional county boundaries in the interests of administrative convenience, which takes no cognizance of historic loyalties) there is an abundance of stone and, in the Middle Ages and for some time after, there were almost limitless quantities of the best of all our woods for building: oak. It is true that this region is poorly off for limestone and that most of the sandstones are Triassic, which, for all the charm of their colours (and these range delightfully – New Red Sandstone is of course by no means always red), seldom stand up well to the English weather. On the other hand, because of their comparative softness, especially at the quarry (for like all sedimentary rocks they harden somewhat on exposure to the air), these sandstones are easy to work. It is therefore a matter of some surprise to find that in the West Midlands, where, as was so often the case, stone and wood were both readily available locally, it was the oak which was frequently preferred.

With a few minor exceptions the churches, by the end of the twelfth century, were all built of stone, and so were the castles; but until the last quarter of the seventeenth century it is probably no exaggeration to say that in the counties of the West Midlands towns, villages, farmhouses, cottages, and all working buildings such as barns and mills, were predominantly if not wholly timber-framed as a matter of course. It was only the big country houses, starting with Compton Wynyates, dating

1 Leigh Court Barn, Worcestershire, which it is hoped will be taken into care by the Department of the Environment.

from the early years of Henry VIII, which were usually built of brick or stone; but even among these there are exceptions, like Pitchford Hall near Shrewsbury and Grimshaw Hall at Knowle.

Documentation of timber-framed buildings is notably scarce, but it seems highly probable that the earliest were of the cruck type. Perhaps no finer example of a cruck building can be found anywhere than Leigh Court Barn, five miles south-west by west of Worcester; see photograph 1. From outside, unhappily, it looks somewhat dilapidated; but within it is superb. There are no fewer than eleven pairs of crucks, most of which are about 35 feet long. A few stop at a high collar-beam a little below the ridge, including, necessarily, the two end-pairs, as the end-gables are half-hipped. The oak is its natural colour, and not one of these gigantic crucks, which are probably at least 650 years old, has needed to be renewed. This barn, which is 34 feet wide and over 150 feet long, is no longer thatched, and there is a clear distinction here between

2 Bishop Percy's House, Cartway, Bridgnorth, Salop. Built 1580.

the walls and the roof. The infilling for the walls is now mostly brick nogging, but in places the original broad oak slithers still survive.
The roof today is entirely red tiles, partly old hand-made tiles of a lovely terracotta shade, but partly less red – and less good – renewals. This is still a working barn, filled with corn in the fullness of summer, which is as it should be: but so remarkable a structure should also be a national monument, and receive a grant for very necessary repairs.

Cruck-framed buildings are better seen today in the West Midlands, and especially in Herefordshire, than anywhere else, but even here the numbers that have survived are comparatively few. Vertical posts replaced the curving crucks and the large majority of timber-framed buildings in this part of England belong to what is known as the post-and-truss type. Each pair of posts supports a truss, which is a strong triangular frame. The trusses, like the crucks, are linked horizontally by purlins and a ridge-beam, and in addition the tops of the posts are joined by wall-plates. Here was a skeleton easily strong enough to support the common rafters of the roof, and even, indeed, as can still be seen quite often in Shropshire and Herefordshire, a covering of heavy stone slates.

In houses two or three storeys high the ground storey posts carry not the roof trusses but the floor-joists of the storey above, which often project, to form what is known as a jetty. This may occur on one elevation alone, or on several: occasionally, as on the charming little gatehouse at Lower Brockhampton near Bromyard, all four faces are jettied. Where an old house has three storeys, a double jetty is no rarity. Bishop Percy's House at the lower end of Cartway, Bridgnorth, built in 1580, is a characteristic example; see photograph 2.

The subsidiary timbers on the face of a timber-framed building were arranged in a great many different ways. The simplest, and also the most dignified, is a succession of closely spaced verticals, more common in East Anglia and the five south-eastern counties than in the West Midlands, but well seen, for example, in Malt Mill Lane at Alcester. Broader panels were more economical, since laths and plaster cost much

3 The barn in the outer court of Kenilworth Castle, Warwickshire, *circa* 1565–70. In the care of the Department of the Environment.

less than oak. But in the West Midlands, where rectangular and even square panels are not at all unusual, those who could afford it were often tempted, under Elizabeth I and James I especially, to add within these panels patterns of a purely decorative character. Bishop Percy's House has star-patterns, ogees and herringbones; other houses have circles, diamonds, lozenges, criss-crosses, trefoils and quatrefoils. The barn built about 1565–70 by Robert Dudley, Earl of Leicester, in the outer court of Kenilworth Castle has along its side-wall a specially stylish variation: cusped ogees of a very uncommon design; see photograph 3. The infilling here is brick, as often in Warwickshire; sometimes, however, (although not here) the brick nogging was a later introduction, replacing the original wattles and daub or laths and plaster.

The West Midlands, with Cheshire and Lancashire, is the great region for 'black and white', in contrast to Eastern and South-eastern England, where oak is usually left in its grey-brown natural state, while the plaster panels may be off-white, buff, pale ochre or, in Suffolk, pink. It is known that in Shropshire, in 1574, Sir Thomas Kytson paid for the whitening of the plaster panels of his house and for the blackening of the timber work. But with what? Tar and pitch, distilled from coal, were not available until the nineteenth century and earlier materials, charcoal or lamp black, were not durable. There can be no doubt that the 'black and white' which we see today in the West Midlands (and in Cheshire) is very largely if not wholly Victorian. It was a Victorian fashion which exercised so great an appeal that, even now, it is not difficult in this part of the country to find houses with brick walls which have been carefully whitened and blackened to fulfil their 'magpie' aspirations.

In isolation 'black and white' is undoubtedly effective. But it is not a good mixer, and into towns it can introduce a note of stridency which is not kind to neighbouring buildings in brick or stone. For my part, therefore, the recent tendency, seen for example at the Reader's House and at the Feathers Hotel in Ludlow, to remove the blackening and to restore to the oak its natural colour marks a welcome swing of the pendulum of taste.

In the field of brickwork, the West Midlands were late starters. For a number of reasons, of which the most important was the relative scarcity of stone compared with the West, bricks were made and used in all the counties of eastern England, from Kent, Sussex and Hampshire to the East Riding of Yorkshire, and especially in East Anglia, long before they were to be seen in the profusely wooded sandstone counties of the West. In none of our five counties is there any substantial brick building earlier in date than Compton Wynyates, mentioned above, and even here all the roofs are of stone, not tiles. Brick remained an unusual material in the West Midlands, a perquisite of the well-to-do, until after the Restoration.

Of the few fine houses dating from the early seventeenth century, the grandest of which is readily accessible to all: Aston Hall in Birmingham, built between 1618 – 1635. Ingestre Hall, erected about the same time, must once have been almost equally impressive. Ludstone Hall,

4 Ludstone Hall, Claverley, Salop.
Privately owned.

Claverley, set within a moat in an exquisite garden, is smaller; see photograph 4. This charming Jacobean house, with Dutch-type gables and beautiful chimney-stacks, is built of the two-inch bricks which were characteristic of the time; the roof of dark red tiles has been renewed, but not obtrusively. My only reservation applies to many brick houses in the West Midlands: the dressings are of red sandstone, which does not make nearly such an effective foil to red brick as the lighter-toned limestones, Portland above all.

The chief surviving brick houses of this area which are, in part at least, earlier than any of these are, apart from Compton Wynyates, all in Shropshire: Plaish Hall, Upton Cressett and Whitton Court. Plaish Hall, dating from about 1540, is specially notable for its finely moulded brick chimney-stacks, a most unusual feature in this part of England. Whitton Court has a picture-book front facing the garden (and a twenty-mile view stretching to the Malverns). Worcestershire has one remarkable early brick house, Westwood Park near Droitwich; but although the centre, built as a shooting lodge, was complete by 1600, the four wings attached diagonally to the corners of the original house to produce a mansion quite unlike any other in the country, were not added until the 1660s (although fortunately in a perfectly harmonious, so by then old-fashioned style). In Warwickshire, Castle Bromwich Hall belongs to much the same two dates; Charlecote Park has a lovely Elizabethan gatehouse but the brickwork of the mansion decayed so badly that most of it, like much of the interior, is today nineteenth century work.

Notable brick houses of Charles II's time include Soulton Hall near Wem, Weston Park in Staffordshire, Holme Lacy near Hereford and Honington Hall in Warwickshire. For Weston – and I dare say for the others, too – the bricks were made from clay dug on the estate, which also supplies from its own quarry the stone for the dressings and from its own woods the timber for the joinery; a perfect illustration of how people, even quite grand people, nearly always built with the materials closest at hand. Unfortunately at Weston, at the beginning of the nineteenth century, the whole house was rendered, presumably in an attempt to make it look more fashionable, at a time when stone, or at least the semblance of stone, was almost *de rigueur* in the most polite circles. To provide a key for the stucco the bricks were all scored. Shortly before the last war the stucco was removed, to the great benefit of the house's appearance; but the damage to the brickwork is visible.

Nearly all the finest brickwork of the West Midlands belongs to the eighteenth century. In all our five counties, even Herefordshire, which comes into the picture exceptionally late, brick at last became the usual building material for 'middling' houses and even, over some parts of our area, for cottages too. It was indeed, as the century advanced, the aristocracy who tended wherever possible to reject brick, and especially red brick, 'the colour of which is fiery . . . and in summer has an appearance of heat that is very disagreeable', as Isaac Ware had written, with more pretension than good sense, in 1756. But, except by the

5 The Town Hall, Tamworth,
Staffordshire. Built 1701.

addition of stucco, as at Weston Park, the rejection of red brick would have been virtually impossible over most of the West Midlands before the Victorian period, because there were only a very few places where bricks of other colours could be made with the clays then exploitable. (Brown bricks were made at Stone: mottled orange at Madeley). The pleasures, and they are many, are in fact almost all among the reds.

Brickwork in the West Midlands did not achieve the subtleties of the South-east, where not only are rubbed and gauged bricks to be seen in profusion but the most refined carving too, demanding, for some of the designs, prodigies of skill. Yet if the best brickwork of, say, Bewdley or Pershore cannot equal that of Farnham or Chichester, the general impression made by these towns is delightful. And many more can be added: the Georgian brick buildings of Worcester and Warwick, Shrewsbury and Ludlow, Whitchurch and Lichfield, and are among the greatest ornaments of these towns, especially when their sash-framed windows keep their glazing bars, which are visually of vital importance, and are painted white, as they almost always should be. At Tamworth the little Town Hall of 1701 with walls of diapered brickwork (not very common in the West Midlands), supported on stone arcades which have fortunately never been filled in, adds a note of great distinction to the town centre; see photograph 5.

Brick now became the favourite material even for churches and chapels, while the number of country houses built of it is too great even to mention them individually. But none, perhaps, is more pleasing than one of the first: Hanbury Hall, also completed in 1701, see photograph 6. This fine Worcestershire house, a property of the National Trust, is built of bright red local brick of fine quality, with dressings of dun-coloured Triassic sandstone, also local, and white painted wooden 'trim', including the delightful central cupola with the clock. Some idea of the high quality of these 1700 bricks can be had by comparing them with those made in the Victorian period for the piers of the forecourt.

6 Hanbury Hall, Worcestershire.
Completed 1701. Owned by the National
Trust.

The chief contribution of the nineteenth century was the outcome of the
mechanical ingenuity of that brilliantly inventive age. Before the
Victorian period the tough shales and mudstones of the Coal Measures,
although present in abundance in Staffordshire and to some small extent
in Shropshire and Worcestershire too, could hardly be used for
brickmaking. The invention of machines for grinding these clays was a
revolutionary step, and other machines dried the clay, squeezed it through
a mill and thence carried it on rollers to a table on which it could be cut
into the required sizes by means of wires hung from a mechanical frame.
Mass production had arrived, and the aesthetic results were in many ways
disastrous. But it was these processes which gave us the well-known
'Staffordshire blues', so much in demand for engineering projects of all
kinds and often to be seen in the West Midlands wherever there is still a
railway. These blue-grey bricks, fired at a very high temperature (up to
$1200°C$), are exceedingly strong; but they have sometimes been
employed for ordinary building purposes too, and can give real pleasure,

especially if used in combination with dressings of red brick or stone and plenty of white paint on doors, window-frames and cornices. Visually they are far more pleasing than the harsh reds of the bricks produced at places a little outside our area, such as Ruabon and Accrington, from clays of much the same age and character.

Martin Opie

'Just dust and pitch' were the headlines in January last year following an inspection of the carved barge boards of the Old House in the heart of Hereford's central High Town. A mild fate this might be thought for a building which between the years 1810–1854 survived the efforts of that august body 'the Paving, Repairing, Cleaning and Lighting Commissioners' to secure its demolition for widening the street. Indeed on 9 June 1816, one form of public participation is evident from the following extract from their Minute Book which solicits public support:

'Resolved that it is the opinion of this meeting that the old building in the parish of St Peter, called by the name of the Butcher Row, are a great annoyance, and that it would add much to the ornament and convenience of the said City to take the said buildings down; that for the purpose of defraying the expense thereof it is expedient to solicit voluntary contributions from the inhabitants of the said City and neighbourhood.'

The Old House, see photograph 1, is now all that remains of a group of ten or twelve buildings of the same style, although not so substantial, called 'The Butcher Row' which had stood on the site from their origin in the tudor period. The date of 1621 is clearly borne on a shield held by an angel, although some experts consider it to be older by some fifty years.

Butcher Row is believed to have been the work of John Abell. This village carpenter of Sarnesfield, born in 1570 and later made one of His Majesty's carpenters by King Charles I after his improvement of a mechanism for grinding corn during the siege of Hereford in 1645, is well known in connection with the timber houses of the Hereford area. Amongst his better known and documented works are Market Houses for Brecon, 1624, Leominster, 1634, and Kington, 1654, and the restoration of many county churches.

The Old House, as its name implies, started life as a dwelling. Tradition later associates it with the headquarters of the Butcher Guild, of which it bears the Arms (crossed slaughter axes) believed to have been used in

1 The Old House, Hereford as it appears in a lithograph dated 1 February 1830.

Hereford without authority. The barge boards which are carried on projecting plates and purlins and which give protection from rain to the upper walls, are here elaborately carved and decorated, exhibiting the highly developed skill and imagination of the carver. Being part of a row, the eastern and western ends of the House were not fenestrated originally and that now in existence dates from 1884 when the building was purchased by the Worcester Bank for their own use. A stable period in the building's history followed and in 1929 Lloyds Bank, who had taken over the business, subsequently made a gift of the Old House to the City of Hereford. Since then it has been retained as a museum, essentially unaltered except for the incorporation of fifteenth and seventeenth century fireplaces in place of those of more recent origin. During a routine repair and redecoration of the Old House in 1973 a close and detailed inspection was made of the fabric. When the full extent of decay was realised, action was clearly needed and soon if further damage to the fabric of the building was to be avoided.

The first and probably most difficult part of any restoration project is to seek out advice of a quality and experience appropriate to the task. Regrettably local enquiries of a number of firms elicited no satisfactory response and indications were that in the South of England a number of firms might be capable of undertaking the re-carving and restoration. The majority of firms approached were unwilling or unable to assist until

2 The barge boards displaying an advanced state of deterioration.

Mr Harrison of Herbert Read Limited came to our aid and whose wise counsel has been invaluable throughout the restoration which is now nearing completion.

On inspection the woodwork was found to be predominantly in oak with some renovations both in oak and softwood. Over the years the weather had split the face of the carved work allowing water to enter and cause added damage through wet rot. The combined activities of decay and wet rot resulted in the disappearance of more and more of the carving until finally on areas of many of the barge boards, and particularly on the inverted centre newels, it had disappeared completely. Repeated applications of tar to protect the woodwork had created its own special problems, see photograph 2; by forming a complete coating over the surface which had split, water had penetrated behind the tar causing wet rot which continued unchecked and unnoticed behind the apparently undamaged face of the carving. Although firm evidence does not exist, early photography appears to indicate a relatively rapid deterioration over twenty-five to thirty years and it is thought that splits in the tar coating in low temperatures may well have been sealed over through sun action, trapping moisture behind the coating and intensifying the action of decay.

Damp penetration through the mortar soffit to the tile verge, in direct contact with the wood, had also been a major contributing factor. Due to the moisture retention of the mortar, the top edge of the barge boards remained almost continuously wet, further assisting the formation of wet rot. The grain of the wood from which the angels were carved was at an angle of 30 degrees from the vertical, presenting the grain at its most vulnerable, and consequently the angels had suffered and even those replaced on the east gable in the Victorian restoration were cracked from the top, it only being a matter of time before the whole face would split away. The gable-end inverted newels had suffered by being directly beneath the valleys between the gables and the lead valleys had deteriorated with more end grain water penetration. Whole sections of the bunches of grapes had split away due to the presentation of end grains to the weather, although at some time past lead leaves, cut to fit tightly round the stems and protect the top surface, had helped to preserve the remains of the carving. Unfortunate also was the character of certain of the restoration work in Victorian times where the gaunt and earnest heads replaced the characteristically cherubic and cheerful faces of the period.

The extent of decay and the very exposed nature of the work seemed to indicate the necessity of total replacement and re-carving. Replacement in oak was not advocated in these particular circumstances as Burma teak is a hardier and more enduring timber for such exposed conditions, the closeness of grain proving of particular advantage given the fineness of detail of the carving. This alternative, of course, could not have been considered had it not been for the black staining and painting of the remainder of the framing of the Old House which it was decided should be retained as a permanent feature and now a part of the tradition. Oak has of course been used where certain of the existing work has been capable of repair but, having survived for over two hundred and fifty years, nothing but the best was thought to be good enough.

Other action aimed at extending the life of new work included sealing all end grain and where possible capping it with lead; the heads of angels, leaves of the bunches of grapes and top surfaces of inverted newel posts are also to be treated in this way, in addition to the more traditional use of lead flashings at verges and the abutments. Some consideration was given to the possibility of taking moulds of repaired barge boards, newels, etc. and casting replacements in modern materials, but this was generally considered to be impractical, either because their durability could not be sufficiently guaranteed or because the cost or weight of such materials was excessive in the circumstances. Moreover, the clarity of the carving which did remain was either partially obscured by the coating of tar, or the tar itself was merely a mould of an earlier profile now decayed. To remove the tar was to risk destruction of the remaining legend, but retention would have so detracted from the quality of any subsequent moulding that this had to be ruled out.

Estimates were received and approved, work of replacement was put in hand, and with scaffolding in place the first sections were removed. This activity engendered the usual degree of local interest, and an opportunity for effective participation by the Hereford Civic Trust evolved. Natural concern arose over the absolute necessity for replacement, the interpretation of design, historical integrity, the character of the new carving and an understandable wariness of its 'crispness', perhaps best evidenced by the Victorian work on the east gable. Whilst removal enabled the estimate of necessary work to be 'firmed up' parallel investigations were made into a process of epoxy resin impregnation originated in Holland. Knowledge of some experimental work involving this process emerged from the Department of the Environment following

3 The master carver at work.

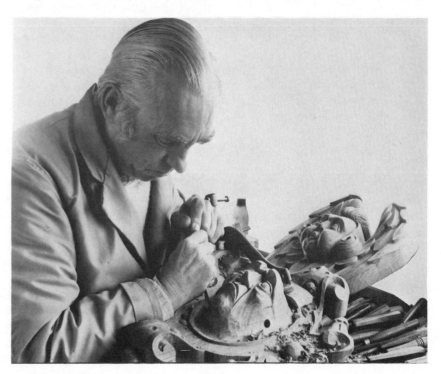

a series of enquiries initiated into the available techniques for wood hardening. Initial response from the specialists first suggested that total penetration by the liquid could be achieved *in situ* by surface application on the untreated and generally firm rear surfaces of the barge boards. A different epoxy formulation could then be injected behind the pitch coating where friable timber, capable of absorbing the first application, did not exist. Enthusiasm was reinforced by two convincing samples of timber, one untreated and in an advanced state of decay, the other blackened by the process of impregnation, but whilst clearly formerly in a similar state of decay, the treated sample was now hard, strong and apparently durable. The technique essentially relied upon the porosity of decayed material to absorb the resin by repeated and continuous application until total penetration was achieved.

The epoxy resin formation was of a modulus of elasticity similar to that of the oak and being an inert material in essence was unlikely to set up internal stress at the point of bond with sound timber. Sound timber though is not inert and it was considered that to cover both the problems of the existing moisture in the good timber and the difficulties of totally preventing any moisture from entering in the future, that only the top, front face and the bottom of the barge boards should be treated. This raised the question, at least in our own minds, of whether the bond would be effective, given that, unequal stresses on both sides of the timber, could be caused by exposure to sun and weather and as a result of the different thermal characteristics of the treated and untreated timber. The specialists did not share our misgivings and of course they may well be right.

Mindful of the cellular structure of oak, a test was called for and a section of barge board at the workshops was selected, thoroughly treated on both faces, and after the required curing time, subsequently cut through to assess penetration. This was complete in the decayed areas but virtually non-existent where the timber was sound. Clearly penetration through the rear sound face of the timber was impossible. It was acknowledged that penetration would be better if the external tar coating were removed but as previously stated this would be impractical and the suggestion of finely perforating the coating to allow penetration was rejected as unreliable. A further suggestion that, the barge boards be edge drilled at close intervals to increase penetration, was thought likely to do more harm than good. At the same time, a piece of test carving had been produced which attested the skill and sensitivity of the firm's master carver, Mr Leslie Jewell, see photograph 3. Taking all sides of the problem into account the original intention to carve new woodwork putting the original on display was decided upon as the more equable answer for both the ancient woodwork and the Old House itself. Whilst epoxy impregnation undoubtedly has a significant part to play in restoration work involving timber, this was a specific task for which the technique was not originally developed, and where full reliability could not be absolutely assured. It may well be that this treatment can play a part in the restoration of the pieces for display and this is currently under investigation by Nick Dove the City Museum Curator.

4 The laminating of the teak for the centre newels.

We were delighted, however, that the barge boards from the west gable, south side, were in good enough condition to put back on the Old House so these were stripped of their paint and the minimum of restoration work carried out, this being confined mainly to fitting new tenons to allow the wood to be correctly fitted into the top and bottom newels. However the bottom edge of one of the barge boards had totally decayed and, considering that these old barge boards linked up on the same elevation with new carved work the decayed timber was cut off and a new piece of oak jointed to the original barge board using four hidden tenons and carved to complete the original pattern and strap work. A localised application of epoxy impregnation is however intended for the bottom edge of the other preserved original barge board to increase its resistance to future attack and thereby to prolong its life. It was interesting, whilst stripping the paint, to notice some of the previous colour schemes, only comparatively recently did the black appear; at one time, there was even a good sky blue. It also seems that the original woodwork was put up unpainted and it was only when this became quite deeply weathered that the first protective coatings were applied. In order to fill the eroded soft parts of the grain of the wood, and also, no doubt, the splits and shakes that had appeared, a thick putty-like substance had been applied to the surface of the timber which was built up to bring back some of the sharpness of the original carving.

Teak of the correct dimensions for the centre newels and some of the gable-end newels was not available and these were laminated three times, see photograph 4, for the centre newels and twice for the gable-end newels. It was decided not to depend on the glue joint alone, and false tenons were let in across the joint plane and pinned with teak pins so that if anything did happen to the glue the laminations would still be held. In many of the gable-end newels it was noticed that rot had started in the bottom of the mortice so the new mortices were shaped to allow the water to run off.

It was also interesting to find that the cherub on the west gable of the

5 Angel with shield in the centre gable, bearing the date 1621, awaiting the skill of the carver.

6 The apprentice carver undertaking the strap work and scroll work.

south side, and the cartouche with the devil's head on the west gable of the north side, were both of softwood and therefore probably copies of the originals. Fortunately there was just enough detail on the originals to conclude that the copies were probably quite accurate and therefore formed the basis for the new carving. The Victorian heads to the cherubs with shields in the centre gables of the north and south sides, had already begun to split where the rain was entering the end grain and so the opportunity was taken to replace these heads with something probably closer to the original, see photograph 5. Except for the heads, both these cherubs were in quite sound condition so, all that was required was a new piece of oak let into the back for strengthening, with a further piece for taking the false tenons let into the sloping face of the centre newels.

Wherever any restoration work was carried out the new oak was selected for configuration and direction of grain so that it would be as compatible as possible with the timber with which it was to be integrated. Although

7 The restoration work completed.

the idea was to carve these new boards whilst there was still enough detail on the originals to build up a fairly accurate picture of the carving, every carver creates an individual piece of work even if he is trying to make a copy. We considered it essential to allow Mr Jewell, the master carver, to create his own interpretations and use his individual techniques to make sure that these were not mechanical copies but were very much a piece of living carving in the tradition of the original work. Roger Hill, the apprentice, carved the strap work, see photograph 6, and scroll work boards, and although they afforded little scope for individuality, it has been interesting to see his confidence and ability as a carver developing. Many of the small details on the animals and particularly the treatment of the features of the dragons on the two outer pairs of boards on the north side, and the allegorical beasts in the centre pair on the south side, follow as closely as possible to the original. The tone of the muscle, shape of the claw, expression on the face and the treatment of the bodies, are all the carver's own contribution to the final form of the work, achieved from years of experience and a deep knowledge of carved woodwork of the same period. In a continuing cycle of change, the new work, see photograph 7, can now be seen alongside the preserved gable and the Victorian east gable, the best of the original carving not re-used being retained for exhibition within the Old House in its role as a museum.

Martin Opie wishes to express his thanks to Mr Harrison of Herbert Read Limited, St Sidwell's Art Works, Odams Wharf, Ebford, Exeter, and Nick Dove, City Museum Curator at Hereford.

Barrie Trinder

Iron has been used in building since the late Middle Ages, and in some of its various forms it is still a vital element in twentieth century architecture, but its most significant applications occurred during the period of the Industrial Revolution. Many of the most memorable structures of early industrial civilisation – bridges, textile mills, warehouses, railway stations – were essentially iron structures. Iron was used extensively in the creation of Victorian pleasure resorts, and in those parts of Britain where it was made and fabricated, it was used for a multitude of minor architectural purposes, in cottages, chapels, pubs and shops.

In the twentieth century iron is most commonly used in building in the form of mild steel, a material developed by Henry Bessemer in the middle of the nineteenth century. Prior to that time it was used in the form of either wrought iron or cast iron, and it is with these materials, particularly the latter, that this article is concerned. Wrought iron is a commercially pure form of iron, containing very little of other elements. It is easily forged and shaped when hot, and is strong in tension but weak in compression. Cast iron is an alloy of iron and other elements, particularly carbon. It is strong in compression but weak in tension. It cannot be forged, but can be cast into intricate shapes when in a molten state. In Britain since the sixteenth century, cast iron, in the form of pig iron, has been the first product of the iron-making process, being smelted from the ore on a relatively large scale in a blast furnace. Wrought iron was a secondary product, the result of decarburizing pig iron in a forge, which consisted initially of two separate hearths, the finery and the chafery; from the late eighteenth century puddling furnaces were used. Until the mid-eighteenth century production of iron in Britain was restricted by the necessity to use charcoal as a fuel at all stages of production, but gradually means were found of substituting mineral fuels. In 1709 at Coalbrookdale in Shropshire Abraham Darby first successfully smelted iron ore using coke as a fuel, and by the 1750s teething troubles with this process had been overcome and it was being widely used. After a series of partially successful experiments by others, Henry Cort in 1784 devised the puddling process by which wrought iron could be manufactured from pig iron without the use of charcoal. At the same time the application of the steam engine in ironworks, and its use in the mines which supplied them with raw materials, together with improvements in transport systems, greatly enlarged the capacity of the British iron industry. Between 1750 – 1806 production of pig iron increased approximately tenfold, from 26 000 tons per year to 258 000 tons, a figure which had soared to 2 700 000 by 1852.

Before the blast furnace was introduced into Great Britain about 1500, cast iron was made only by accident, when one of the small bloomery furnaces used for making iron by direct reduction from the ore became overheated. By the mid-sixteenth century ironmasters were learning to use cast iron, and at many blast furnaces some of the iron was used for making castings rather than for conversion to wrought iron. Some sixteenth century grave slabs survive in the Weald. The earliest example in the West Midlands is the tomb of Robert Steward at Burrington Church, Herefordshire, dated 1619, and doubtless one of the products of the nearby Bringewood ironworks. Another early use of cast iron was in the form of firebacks, slabs of iron which protected the masonry of large open fireplaces. Both grave slabs and firebacks were often decorated, at first with simple devices such as a rope impressed in the mould, but later with quite elaborate heraldic displays. Many sixteenth and seventeenth century castings are very crude – the lettering on grave slabs for example is often exceedingly muddled – but they do nevertheless indicate a first appreciation of the decorative qualities of cast iron.

In 1708 the Quaker ironmaster Abraham Darby leased the small furnace at Coalbrookdale and the following year succeeded in smelting iron ore with coke instead of charcoal. What is of more significance for the application of iron in architecture in the West Midlands is that Darby was essentially an iron founder, concerned with the making and sale of castings rather than with the production of pig iron for sale to forgemasters. His main trade was in domestic holloware, but by the early 1720s his successors were producing castings for architectural purposes.

In 1721 two firebacks were sold to a customer in Kington, Herefordshire, and a consignment of cast iron bannisters worth nearly £17 was despatched to Bristol. The first recorded use of cast iron railings in Great Britain was in 1714 when railings for St Paul's Cathedral were produced at a Sussex foundry. By the 1730s, large orders for such railings were being supplied from Coalbrookdale for the Herefordshire estates of Edward Harley, for the hospital at Preston-on-the-Weald Moors in Shropshire, and for William Donne of Bristol. Unfortunately the detailed accounts of the Coalbrookdale ironworks for the middle decades of the eighteenth century no longer survive, but there is ample evidence to suggest that the production of castings for architectural purposes was an important and increasing part of the foundry's trade.

Between 1777 – 1781 the world's first iron bridge was erected across the River Severn near Coalbrookdale. The third Abraham Darby was primarily responsible for its construction, although the initial designs had been prepared by the Shrewsbury architect Thomas Farnolls Pritchard. Pritchard had many connections with the ironmasters of the Severn Gorge, having carried out commissions for several of them. He had also ordered cast iron firegrates from the Coalbrookdale ironworks for some of his other jobs, at least one of which still survives at Shipton Hall in the Corvedale. The Iron Bridge quickly became a spectacle which attracted many visitors to Shropshire, but for well over a decade it was a solitary curiosity. It was not until the mid-1790s that further iron bridges were built. This was a time of great advance in the structural use of iron, which saw also the first iron aqueduct, and the first major structural applications of iron in buildings.

The first structural use of cast iron in buildings was in the forms of columns supporting galleries, a use which may perhaps date from as early as the first decade of the eighteenth century, but which certainly did not become widespread until much later. When the Bishop of Lichfield preached at the consecration of George Steuart's Church of All Saints at Wellington, Shropshire in July 1790 he referred to the iron pillars supporting the gallery as if they were something of a novelty. The use of iron framing originated in textile mills, and was stimulated by the need to reduce the fire hazard in such buildings. The first water powered cotton mill was erected at Cromford, Derbyshire, by Richard Arkwright in 1771. It was the prototype for many other multi-storey cotton mills, with load-bearing masonry walls, and wooden floors supported by wooden beams and upright columns. The application of iron in the construction of such mills was due principally to two men, William Strutt, a member of a Derbyshire cotton spinning family, and Charles Bage, a Shrewsbury wine merchant, whose family originated in Derbyshire. The two kept up a regular correspondence, and had contacts with many of the leading figures in the Midlands of the time, including Erasmus Darwin and Thomas Telford. In 1792–93, Strutt used two rows of cast iron columns in a six-storey cotton mill in Derby, in which the floors were carried on segmental brick arches, and the timber cross beams were encased in plaster as a means of protecting them from fire. Strutt used a similar form of construction in a small warehouse at Milford, Derbyshire, erected at the same period, and in the West Mill at Belper which was completed in 1795. Unfortunately none of these buildings now survives.

In 1796 the flax spinner John Marshall of Leeds, and his partners the brothers Benjamin and Thomas Benyon whose home was in Shropshire, decided to build a new flax mill in Shrewsbury, following the destruction by fire of one of their Leeds mills. Charles Bage entered their partnership, and designed a mill with both upright columns and cross beams of cast iron, and floors, like those in Strutt's mills, carried on segmental brick arches. In determining the dimensions of the cruciform section upright columns of the mill, Bage made use of experiments on the structural properties of cast iron carried out by William Reynolds at the Ketley ironworks in connection with the design of Thomas Telford's aqueduct at Longdon on Tern on the Shrewsbury Canal. By using iron, Bage was able to construct a building with a width of nearly forty feet, considerably greater than that of most traditional textile mills, which rarely exceeded twenty-eight feet. The Shrewsbury mill, situated in Ditherington, a northern suburb of the town, was erected with

1 The Maltings, Ditherington, Shrewsbury. Completed in 1797 as a flaxmill. This was the first building in the world to utilise cast iron beams and columns, resulting in a fire-proof construction. The columns on the right have forked tops to support lineshaft bearings.
Interior view of top floor showing central line of iron columns.

2 North Mill, Belper, Derbyshire, completed in 1804, is one of the most sophisticated of the early iron-framed multi-storey factory buildings.

astonishing speed, the main structure being completed by September 1797, the parts having been cast by the local ironfounder William Hazledine. It is now accepted that this mill, which happily still survives, was the first wholly iron-framed multi-storey building. It was not however iron-framed in the sense that modern architects would use the term, for the iron members sustained only the floors, and the walls still carried their own weight and much of that of the roof.

Bage's mill at Shrewsbury was the pattern for at least seven other mills built before 1807. In 1799–1801 a massive seven-storey iron-framed mill, forty-seven feet wide and two hundred and thirty-eight feet long was built in Salford for Messrs Phillips, Wood and Lee. For many years this was believed to be the first iron-framed textile mill. It was unfortunately destroyed by bombing during the Second World War. In 1802 Bage and the Benyon brothers built a new mill in Leeds, possibly the first to have a cast iron-framed roof, and in 1803–04 they constructed

a second iron-framed mill in Castlefields, Shrewsbury. At the same time in Derbyshire William Strutt built the North Mill at Belper, which, apart from the Ditherington mill in Shrewsbury, is the only iron-framed mill from this period to survive. Of the mills from a slightly later period which still stand is the Stanley Mill near Stroud, Gloucestershire, of 1812 – 13, for which the splendidly elaborate castings were supplied by the Level Ironworks near Dudley. The majority of textile mills of the early nineteenth century were not iron-framed, for the smaller type of mill with wooden beams and pillars seems at that time to have been a more economic structure to erect and operate, and a measure of protection against fire could be obtained by encasing timber structural members with plaster. It was not until the 1830s when increased demands for cotton thread were created by investment in power looms by weaving manufacturers, that the larger iron-framed mill became a thoroughly economic proposition. The slow adoption of iron framing obscured its early history. William Fairbairn, one of the greatest nineteenth century structural engineers and a prolific writer on the uses of iron, knew nothing of the work of Bage and the Strutts, and it was not until the 1940s that the significance of the Ditherington mill was appreciated as the result of the work of an American scholar.

Iron was employed in many other types of large industrial buildings in the early nineteenth century apart from cotton mills. Cast iron columns were often employed to carry dock warehouses, enabling an open, uncluttered working area to be created at ground floor levels. Telford used them at St Katharine Docks, London, in the 1820s, but the most spectacular example of this style of building is without doubt Jesse Hartley's Albert Dock, Liverpool, of 1845. Many of the great dockyard buildings of this period, notably those at Sheerness and Woolwich, also had iron frames, and part of a large smithy from Woolwich awaits re-erection at the Ironbridge Gorge Museum.

The iron-framed textile mill was in many respects the ancestor of the steel-framed skyscraper of the twentieth century, and was a development of major importance in the history of architecture.

There were many other interesting but less epoch-making uses to which iron was put in buildings in the late eighteenth century. Iron railings and balconies became one of the most prominent features of late Georgian and Regency town houses. The architect John Nash pioneered several new uses of iron. In 1805 he used iron arches to form windows to light from above a picture gallery which he created in what had previously been the courtyard of Lord Berwick's mansion at Attingham Park, Shropshire. Like several other architects of the time he employed cast iron doric columns, most notably in the building of the north lodge at Buckingham Palace, and in Carlton House Terrace. He made particularly effective use of the decorative qualities of cast iron in the Royal Pavilion, Brighton, where he erected iron staircases which appear to be made of bamboo. In all of these applications he was to be followed by many later nineteenth century architects.

3 Coach House of The Grange, Coalbrookdale, Shropshire, incorporating cast iron window sills and lintels.

4 Cast iron chimney pots are still common in Coalbrookdale, the seat of the modern British iron industry.

5 Lloyds Bank Chambers, Madeley, Shropshire. Here extensive use has been made of cast iron as a decorative medium.

In areas where iron was manufactured, it was often used very widely indeed, even in the humblest of dwellings. In the Coalbrookdale region of Shropshire it is possible to see cottages with iron lintels over windows and doors, cast iron window frames, iron door steps and iron chimney pots. While iron window frames were quite widely used, the manufacture of such items as lintels and chimney pots seems to have been undertaken to satisfy the needs of a largely local market. Occasional examples of these items can be found throughout the Shropshire coalfield, but the greatest concentration is in the immediate vicinity of the Coalbrookdale ironworks. Cast iron shop fronts such as the extraordinary piece of artistry which adorns the building in Madeley which now houses Lloyds Bank, were also produced in the mid-nineteenth century. While they were offered for sale in ironworks catalogues, they do not seem to have been commonly used outside the ironworking districts.

The standard gauge railways first introduced iron as a building material to most parts of Great Britain. Countless station canopies were carried on cast iron columns, some of them elaborately designed to incorporate company initials or insignia. Outstanding examples which still survive are at Malvern in Worcestershire and Ulverston. Iron was also employed by the railway companies to create totally new kinds of structure, like locomotive roundhouses, or the great terminal stations. Brunel and Wyatt's Paddington of 1854 consists of wrought iron roof members carried on cast iron columns, and Barlow's St Pancras of 1867 is a vast wrought iron arch erected above a vault, which forms the operating surface of the station, the roof of which is supported by six hundred and eighty-eight cast iron columns.

Iron was one of the two principal materials used in the greatest of all Victorian buildings, Joseph Paxton's Crystal Palace, built to house the Great Exhibition of 1851. Paxton's plans were completed only in June 1850, work on the foundations in Hyde Park began in August of the same year, and by 1 May 1851 the whole vast structure was complete and the exhibition ready for opening. The iron was supplied and erected by Messrs Fox and Henderson of Smethwick, and the glass work by Messrs

6 The Crystal Palace, completed in 1851 for the Great Exhibition, demonstrated *par excellence* the opportunities offered by iron for large scale buildings and prefabricated construction.

Chance of Birmingham. The Crystal Palace was a triumph of pre-fabrication, employing over three thousand iron columns and over two thousand cross girders. It seemed to point the way to a whole new pattern of building, and many town halls and corn exchanges of the 1850s were intended to be modelled upon it. In the event, large numbers of them were finally realised as conventional masonry structures in the classical or Gothic style, and buildings which were truly successors to the Crystal Palace did not appear in any great number in Britain until well into the twentieth century.

Iron was still extensively used in Victorian architecture however, cast iron columns being employed in many chapels, market halls, factories and warehouses, and grates and heating stoves being installed in every sort of house from the mansion to the cottage. It was in the architecture of recreation that the ornamental qualities of cast iron were most effectively exploited. The Victorian seaside pier was essentially an essay in cast and wrought iron, often with elements of fantasy about it. Any town or village, inland or coastal, which saw itself as a resort, erected canopies on cast iron columns in front of its principal shops. Iron bandstands decorated many a Victorian park. At Tenbury Wells, Worcestershire, a bath house of highly imaginative Gothic design was constructed in iron with the object of attracting visitors to the spa. With the advent of Bessemer steel in the latterpart of the nineteenth century, cast and wrought iron were used less frequently for structural purposes, although the former is still extensively employed in various ways in contemporary architecture.

Much remains to be discovered about the history of iron in building. It is only in comparatively recent times that the work of William Strutt and Charles Bage has been re-discovered. In the late 1960s a row of millworkers cottages under demolition at Fazeley was found to be of fireproof construction, and in 1973 a stable adjacent to the Ditherington Mill in Shrewsbury was found to have an iron roof and this now awaits re-erection at the Ironbridge Gorge Museum. It is to be hoped that in the near future as a result of both documentary research and detailed field work we shall learn more about the first uses of cast iron columns to support church galleries, about the design and casting of iron grates for Georgian mansions, and about the development of the cast iron window frame.

Architectural Ceramics

Ronald Brunskill

'Architectural ceramics' is the convenient if rather inelegant term for the materials made of baked earth which are used in buildings. Thus bricks, roofing tiles, wall tiles, terra cotta and glazed tiles of various sorts are examples of architectural ceramics. The rapid and widespread adoption of hand made bricks and tiles transformed the Midland Counties during the seventeenth century from a scene of timber frame and thatch to one of brick walls and tiled roofs; the introduction of shale-based and machine-made bricks and tiles during the nineteenth century helped to complete the transformation into the rather harsh but often colourful urban scene which we are beginning to appreciate today; flirtation with terra cotta and wall tiles of various sorts during the past fifty years or so seems likely to give way to a return to the simple, quite basic bricks and tiles which can do so much to relate the often alien forms of modern buildings to urban or rural settings in which they are found.

1 St John's Hospital, Lichfield, founded 1495.

In what is still the standard work on the subject, Nathaniel Lloyd's *History of English Brickwork* it was maintained that the well-made, well-burnt brick is the most durable of all building materials, one which can be produced in an almost infinite variety of forms, colours, and textures, and one which can be used in multitudinous ways. And yet it was many centuries after the departure of those great brickmakers, the Romans, before the value and the versatility of the material was appreciated by builders who were more accustomed to the workability of stone or the flexibility of timber.

The earliest known examples of medieval brickwork in England are in the vicinity of Colchester, in Essex and around the Humber in Yorkshire and Lincolnshire, but the material was used for buildings of high status, such as the Abbey at Little Coggeshall or the Holy Trinity Church at Hull, or for reasons of defence, as at the town walls and gatehouses of Beverley or the tower of Little Wenham Hall. The substantial increase in the use of bricks which took place in the fifteenth century was still generally confined to their use on important buildings such as Tattershall Castle in Lincolnshire built about 1434–1448 or Herstmonceaux Castle in Sussex of about 1440. During the reign of Henry VIII the material became sufficiently popular for Alec Clifton-Taylor to call this period the first great age of English brickwork. The material was held in such high esteem that both Wolsey and Henry himself were happy to have their palaces of bricks, but brickwork was still far from being widely adopted in England either socially or geographically: very few small houses were built wholly of brick during the sixteenth century and even among the larger country houses Plaish Hall, Shropshire of *circa* 1500, and Compton Wynyates, Warwickshire of 1560–67, are exceptional. With the coming of the seventeenth century the spread of brickwork socially from buildings of high status to those of lesser importance and geographically from the Eastern and South-eastern counties to much of the Midlands and the South began to quicken its pace. Now the material was quite commonly adopted for country houses – Aston Hall, Birmingham of 1618–35, is a well known example – and following the restoration its use became very widespread indeed.

During the later years of the seventeenth century Dutch influence was strong and the neat symmetrical houses with their plain brick walls and wide-spreading tiled roofs are amongst the most charming in any town. The memories of fires which had devastated towns such as Warwick or Nantwich and had culminated in the Great Fire of London added the search for fire-resistant materials to the inclinations of fashion. Competition for timber and probably a breakdown of the medieval systems of cultivation of timber for buildings in the face of increased population and improving standards, encouraged the search for alternative building materials. The eighteenth century therefore was a period of almost universal use of brickwork in the Midland Counties when towns such as Bewdley or Shrewsbury, see photograph 2, took on much of their present character. The material became so popular that it was worth taxing, and the Brick Taxes introduced in 1784 and maintained until 1851 led to some detailed modifications in brickwork but seemed to have had little or no effect on the spread of the material

2 A street scene in Shrewsbury.

through the Midlands. At first the tax was levied on each thousand bricks
without limit on the size of an individual brick and some ingenious
brick-makers produced bricks which required gargantuan hands to lay;
these 'Great Bricks' may sometimes be seen in buildings of about 1790;
but later a limit of 150 cubic inches volume before the tax was increased
eliminated the advantage of these freak bricks but still made the
three inch deep brick financially attractive however visually unattractive
it might be.

The nineteenth century saw developments which increased the demand
for bricks but also improved and cheapened their manufacture. The
newly established industries, the vastly increased populations to be
housed, the swiftly spreading railway network all placed demands on the
supplies of building materials which could only be met by use of bricks.
The old techniques whereby brick-earth was dug on the site of the
building, moulded by hand into 'green' bricks, then fired in a clamp
which was made for the purpose and used for the one building enterprise
or in a kiln which was filled, heated, cooled and emptied in a slow
intermittent process, were inadequate for the new demands. The process
of getting the brick-earth was mechanised and concentrated in vast
brickfields. New mechanised methods of grinding and mixing allowed
shaly earths which fired well and produced strong bricks to be used.
Mechanised processes allowed ordinary bricks to be extruded like
tooth-paste in the 'wire-cut' process or hydraulically pressed to produce
the immensely strong bricks for which Staffordshire is so famous.
Then the continuous kilns, such as the Hoffman kiln introduced about
1858, ensured that bricks could be produced by the million to meet
demands which were now being counted by the million.

Most of these bricks were laid in utilitarian structures such as pottery
kilns or railway viaducts which might be no less graceful for being useful.
Many were laid in the economical English Garden Wall bond in the vast
terraces of workers' houses. But large numbers were also laid in the walls
of commercial or institutional buildings in which ingenious bricklaying
was an important part of the design. One aspect of the Gothic Revival

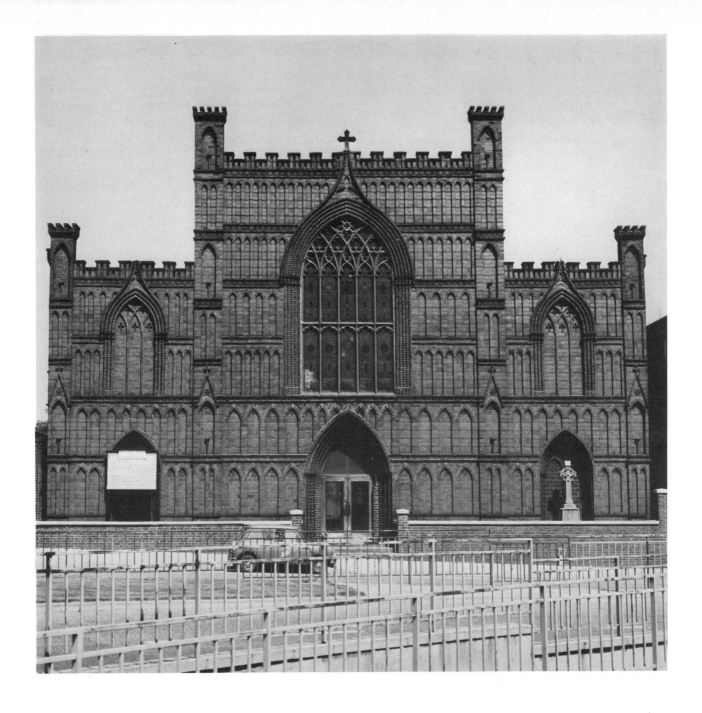

movement called for the use of English Bond and diapered brickwork in buildings such as Stoke-on-Trent Railway Station built in 1847–48. Another allowed the exotic use of hard, pressed, plain and moulded purple bricks in the unique Holy Trinity Church, Newcastle-under-Lyme of 1833–34, see photograph 3. Yet another encouraged the development of polychromatic brickwork whereby blue, yellow, purple or almost black bricks could be mixed with the red to produce effects which can still be quite startling after a century of exposure. Polychromatic brickwork is usually coupled with the Florentine or Sienese Gothic styles and with the pen of Ruskin, though neither the Italian cities nor the Victorian critic would be anxious to claim responsibility for some of the frantic patterns of shops or schools in some of the Midland towns. Nevertheless both utilitarian and decorative brickwork of the nineteenth century is full of interest to the observer who is willing to take note of the care in detailing or bonding taken by the over-worked bricklayers.

The reaction to the hard, precise, mechanical nature of such brickwork included a return to the use of thin hand-made bricks in soft yellowish colours as part of the Vernacular Revival movement. The Bournville Estate outside Birmingham has many charming buildings in this style. The Neo-Georgian, popular between the Wars and exemplified by many a post office and a few of the better employment exchanges, also depended upon skilled brickwork and careful choice of materials. One of the most interesting developments of the period was the use of bricks following the contemporary Dutch fashion in cinemas, especially those of the Odeon chain. The precedents here were almost certainly the buildings designed by W M Dudok, especially his Hilversum Town Hall. In this country they led to the use of large expanses of plain brickwork of thin bricks, often with the horizontal joints raked out to emphasise their proportions, and set against intricate vertical and horizontal bands of projecting or recessed courses, highly ornate, and sometimes cantilevered out on concrete beams as if defying all the traditional rules of bricklaying.

3 Holy Trinity Church, Newcastle-Under-Lyme, 1833–34. Architect the Reverend J Egan.

Over the past thirty years or so brickwork fought a rearguard action against the more fashionable concrete, steel, aluminium and plastic. In some few buildings such as the Keele University chapel its potential was realised but generally bricks were laid for strictly utilitarian purposes in endless miles of dull, uniform, Stretcher Bond in cavity walls. In the most recent years the virtues of bricks as facing or cladding materials over the rivals have been better understood and there are signs that the various materials available will be used in a more restrained manner so once again the durability of a well-made well-burnt brick and the infinite variety of its forms will be virtues understood by designers and craftsmen and enjoyed by the general public who have to use or observe their creations.

Clay tiles have been used for roofing almost as long as bricks have been used for walling, but as they are thinner, used in more exposed situations, liable to damage and decay, few really old roofing tiles have survived. They were used at the earliest period, like bricks, for the superior buildings in places where thatch would not be appropriate and where natural slates or stone tiles were not available. During the eighteenth and nineteenth centuries their use spread all over the Midlands – and many other parts of England – because they were fireproof, relatively permanent, and reasonably cheap. They were used on new buildings and they replaced thatch on old buildings. It has been pointed out that however charming a thatched roof might be and whatever its insulating properties, it was a warm comfortable home for all sorts of vermin, and that, indeed, the health of the ordinary farmer or labourer could not improve until his draughty wattled walls were replaced by brick and his leaky rat and insect-infested roof was replaced by tiles. In the Midlands these were almost entirely plain tiles; the pantiles or other single lap tiles of the North-eastern counties are rarely to be seen. But the plain tiles ranged through generations of irregular, undulating, lichen attracting hand-made tiles before they settled to the neat, precision made and precision laid tiles which dominated the nineteenth century and which still compete to some extent with concrete tiles in the twentieth.

4 Wedgwood Memorial Institute, Burslem,
Stoke-on-Trent, 1863–69.
Architects R Edgar and J L Kipling.

Terra-cotta is a brick-like material which is quite well represented in the
West Midlands. The material had a classical origin and was used
occasionally along with medieval brickwork and quite frequently during
the sixteenth and seventeenth centuries. Its great attraction is the way
in which architectural ornament such as the cusps and crockets of Gothic
or the consoles and modillions of the Renaissance can be produced
without the expense of carving bricks or adding stone dressings. The
blocks are moulded, usually hollow, and then are fired, sometimes fired
twice with a glaze. Unfortunately they never quite match the colour or
texture of the bricks with which they are usually employed and the
terra-cotta blocks almost invariably twist during firing so that they have
to be laid with quite wide joints which, blackening on exposures, give an
unpleasant network running contrary to the architectural lines which the
moulded terra-cotta blocks are intended to reproduce. They are probably
best used sparingly for architectural ornament but quite lavishly to
produce panels or relief decoration. The Wedgwood Memorial

5 Bottle oven, Gladstone Pottery, Longton, Stoke-on-Trent, *circa* 1857.

Institute of 1863 – 69, see photograph 4, in Burslem is a very good example. Sharing some of the virtues and defects both of bricks and terra-cotta blocks are glazed bricks, faience tiles, and decorated flooring tiles. Glazed bricks were especially popular among the designers of public houses in the nineteenth century and most especially at the turn of the century when motifs of the Art Nouveau movement lent themselves particularly well to the material. Faience tiles are made of brick-earth but twice fired, once at a high temperature to solidify the body and then at a lower temperature to fix the glaze. The faience slabs are about 1 inch thick and fixed with mortar or plastic adhesives to a brickwork backing. At one time it was thought that they might be the ideal permanent self-cleansing, non-weathering, maintenance-free cladding material for public buildings, they have generally failed to meet the hopes in one respect or another, though some recent concrete buildings have been quite successfully clad in faience slabs or glazed wall tiles.

The heritage of the West Midlands, in terms of building materials, is quite as rich as that of other regions of England – which means very rich indeed. Many of the materials are based on baked earth and, whether in brick, terra-cotta or tile form, all will repay intelligent observation. The study of the materials has advanced only intermittently and only in certain directions. Examples of most periods survive, are accessible, and will richly repay further study, see photograph 5.

Ronald Brunskill

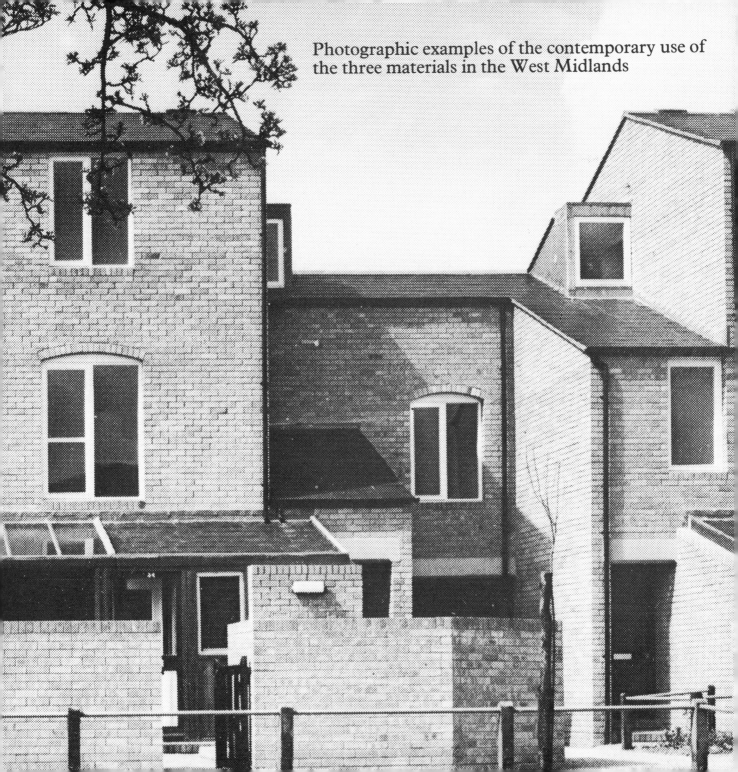

Photographic examples of the contemporary use of the three materials in the West Midlands

1 Annexe to the Concert Hall at the Robert
Jones and Agnes Hunt Orthopaedic
Hospital, Oswestry. This annexe, completed
at the beginning of 1972, was added to an
existing Vic Hallam prefabricated timber
clad concert hall. The annexe is framed in
timber and clad externally in Western Red
Cedar.
Architects: Abbey and Hanson Rowe
and Partners, Shrewsbury.

Photographic examples of the contemporary use of the three materials in the West Midlands

2 Hilda Hayward Swimming Pool built for the Royal Wolverhampton School, Wolverhampton. Completed April 1975. The photograph shows the laminated timber portal arch frames. The roof and gables are in tongued and grooved timber decking. The floor finish is Wolliscrost unglazed ceramic tiles.
Architects: Associated Architects Planning and Landscape Consultants, Birmingham.
Consulting Engineers: Ove Arup and Partners.

Photographic examples of the contemporary use of the three
materials in the West Midlands

3 The office tower of the Birmingham Post
and Mail. The tower, which was completed
in 1966, rises some 200 feet above street level
and is enclosed in a light curtain wall of
aluminium with a silver anodised finish, the
horizontal members having a black anodised
finish.
Architects: The John Madin Design Group,
Birmingham.

Photographic examples of the contemporary use of the three materials in the West Midlands

4 The Locomotive Hall of the Museum of Science and Industry, Birmingham.
The cladding of this building is made of steel covered with vinyl. It was opened in May 1972.
Architects: The City Architect's Department, Birmingham, City Architect W G Reed MCD, BArch, RIBA, MRTPI.

Photographic examples of the contemporary use of the three
materials in the West Midlands

5 The Research and Service Department of
J C Bamford's Manufacturing Plant at
Rocester, near Uttoxeter, Staffs, completed
1969. The aluminium clad fascia is sixty feet
high and more than 0.33 miles in length.
Despite its enormous size the fascia helps the
plant to blend satisfactorily into the
surrounding countryside.
Architect: D B Carton BAHonsArch, RIBA,
Company Architect to J C Bamford.

Photographic examples of the contemporary use of the three
materials in the West Midlands

6 The Masonic Temple, Hagley Road,
Birmingham. This building, completed in
1972, is representative of a fast disappearing
era of 'prestige' building. The bricks, which
are longer and shallower than standard in
order to fit the ten foot module on which the
building is based, were all hand-made at
Coleford in the Forest of Dean. The wide,
raked joints between these buff-brown
bricks gives a rugged appearance and in
massive areas as here gives rise to
monumentality.
Architects: The John Madin Design Group,
Birmingham.

7 Ward's Bridge RSLA Extension, completed 1973. This brick building was built within strict Ministry cost limits and nevertheless displays an imaginative use of Himley Multi-Rustic brick with considerable attention paid to detail. Architects: Wolverhampton Borough Council Architectural Services Department. Director A Chapman ARIBA, MRTPI.

Photographic examples of the contemporary use of the three
materials in the West Midlands

8 The Head Street Development, Pershore, Worcestershire. This recent 'backland' development, rehabilitating and adding to several existing buildings, won an EAHY Civic Trust award 1975. It was particularly praised for its response in both scale and materials to the rest of the old town.
Architects: Darbourne and Darke, London.

Photographic examples of the contemporary use of the three materials in the West Midlands

9 The National Westminster Bank, Stoke-on-Trent, completed in 1972. This redevelopment of a corner site, displaying the use of a dark blue brick made in Mold, North Wales, is one of the finest small-scale recent buildings in the Stoke area.
Architects: Green, Campbell, Wainwright and Partners, Market Drayton.

The Contributors

Dr Derek Linstrum Dip Arch, PhD, FSA, RIBA is Radcliffe lecturer and Director of Conservation studies at the University of York.
He is a noted architectural historian and architectural correspondent to the Yorkshire Post. He is also Chairman of the Yorkshire Committee of European Architectural Heritage Year.

Martin Opie RIBA, RTPI is City Architect and Joint Planning Officer for the City of Hereford. He has worked as an overseas consultant in architecture and planning, has run his own private practice in Kings Lynn 1963–71, and was Assistant County Planning Officer and Head of Design and Conservation for Hertfordshire County Council before taking up his present post in 1974.

Barrie Trinder BA Oxon is Adult Education tutor for historical studies at Salop County Council. He is secretary of the Friends of the Ironbridge Gorge Museum and is on the Executive Board of Ironbridge Gorge Museum as honorary historical adviser.

Dr Ronald Brunskill MA, PhD, ARIBA, FSA is an architect and a senior lecturer in architecture at the University of Manchester.
He is the author of *Illustrated Handbook of Vernacular Architecture* and *Vernacular Architecture of the Lake Counties*. He is President of the Vernacular Architecture Group and Vice-President of the Cumberland and Westmorland Antiquarian and Archaeological Society. Dr Brunskill has recently acted as an assessor in the Heritage Year Awards of the Civic Trust.

Alec Clifton-Taylor FSA is predominantly an author. He is a broadcaster and lectures for the British Council abroad. His classic work for which he is best known is *The Pattern of English Building* which has been re-printed several times. More recently he has written books on English Cathedrals and parish churches. He is collaborating with Dr Brunskill on *English Brickwork* to be published in 1976.

Sir Hugh Casson MA, RA, RDI, RIBA, FSIA is an architect in private practice. He was Professor of Environmental Design at the Royal College of Art 1952–75. He is a member of the Royal Fine Art Commission, the Royal Mint Advisory Committee, the Post Office Design Advisory Committee and is on the Executive and Council of the National Trust. He is a regular contributor to and illustrator for both the lay and technical press and also author of several books. He has lectured on design and conservation throughout Britain and abroad and his watercolours are regularly exhibited.

Heritage Year Awards in the West Midlands

Special Heritage Year Award *Ironbridge Gorge Museum Trust*
Ironbridge, Salop

Schemes of Exceptional Merit *Malt Mill Lane Restoration Project*
Alcester, Warwickshire
Architect: Walter A Thomas of Associated Architects
Feasibility study undertaken by students from Birmingham School of
Architecture

Chesterton Windmill
Warwickshire
Designers: J C E Tainsh, Warwickshire County Architect, in succession
to Eric Davies; Derek Ogen, Millwright (historical research)

Head Street Central Area
(Pershore Central Area Redevelopment)
Pershore, Worcestershire
Architects and Landscape Consultants: Darbourne and Darke

Other Awards *105 – 117 High Street, Coleshill*
Warwickshire
Conservation scheme
Architects: John Tetlow and Partners

Little Virginia
Kenilworth, Warwickshire
Architects: Nichol Thomas Viner Barnwell Partnership

The Old Grammar School House, Kinver
Near Stourbridge, Worcestershire
Architect: John Greaves Smith

Lichfield House (Tudor Cafe)
Lichfield, Staffordshire
Architect: James G Reid

Heritage Year Awards in the West Midlands

The Old House, Shropshire Street
Market Drayton, Salop
Designer and owner: Mr and Mrs G B Hilton

Bear Steps, 8 – 15 St Alkmund's Place
Shrewsbury, Salop
Architect: F W B Charles

Town Hall, Market Street
Tamworth, Staffordshire
Architect: James G Reid

The Shrubbery, Erdington Road
Aldridge, West Midlands
Architects and owner: Ralphs and Mansell

Alton Station
Alton, Staffordshire
Architect: Roderick Gradidge

Lutley Mill, Lutley Lane, Halesowen
Dudley, West Midlands
Architect: L J Southall

Water Tower, Tainters Hill
Kenilworth, Warwickshire
Architect: E R Byron

Hillfield Hall, Hillfield Road
Solihull, West Midlands
Architects: Harper Fairley Partnership

Rock House, Old Hill, Tettenhall
Wolverhampton, West Midlands
Architects: Michael Phillips of Phillips Cutler Phillips Troy

Warrens Hall Park
Rowley Regis, West Midlands
Designer: Directorate of Technical Services of Sandwell Metropolitan
Borough Council

Other Schemes of Merit   *St Thomas' Chapel, Dinham*
Ludlow, Salop

25 St John's, Worcester

Ely Street, Stratford upon Avon

Great Haywood Bridge, Great Haywood
Staffordshire

Hazelhurst Junction, Caldon Canal
Hazelhurst, Staffordshire

The Tudor Garden, Kenilworth Castle
Kenilworth, Warwickshire

Bratch Locks, Wombourn
Wombourn, Staffordshire

Notes

Notes

Production details

Photographs by Colin Reiners
Timber and brick in the West Midlands, 1 2 3 4 5 6
The Old House, Hereford – A Case Study, 7
The Use of Iron in Buildings, 1 2 3 4 5
Architectural Ceramics, 1 2 3 4 5
Photographic examples, 9

Photograph by Richard Einzig
Photographic examples, 8